W9-BXY-711

Migration from Africa

Kevin Cunningham

Raintree

Chicago, Illinois

© 2012 Raintree
an imprint of Capstone Global Library, LLC
Chicago, Illinois

Edited by Louise Galpine, Abby Colich, and Diyan Leake
Designed by Richard Parker
Original illustrations © Capstone Global Library Ltd 2011
Illustrated by Jeff Edwards
Picture research by Mica Brancic

Originated by Capstone Global Library Ltd
Printed and bound in the United States of America,
North Mankato, MN
15 14 13 12 11
10 9 8 7 6 5 4 3 2

Library of Congress Cataloging-in-Publication Data
Cunningham, Kevin, 1966-
   Migration from Africa / Kevin Cunningham.
      p. cm.—(Children's true stories. Migration)
   Includes index.
   Includes bibliographical references and index.
   ISBN 978-1-4109-4072-8 (hc)—ISBN 978-1-4109-4078-0
(pb) 1. African Americans—Migrations—History—Juvenile
literature. 2. African Americans—History—Juvenile literature.
3. Migration, Internal—United States—History—Juvenile
literature. 4. United States—Emigration and immigration—
History—Juvenile literature. I. Title.
   E185.C96 2012
   973'.0496073—dc22   2010039322

Acknowledgments
We would like to thank the following for permission to reproduce photographs: Alamy p. **11** (© Randy Duchaine); Getty Images pp. **5** (Minustah/Sophia Paris), **6** (De Agostini Picture Library/DEA/A. Dagli Orti), **13** (Hulton Archive/Express/William Lovelace), **15** (Redferns/Andrew Lepley), **17** (Popperfoto), **20** (Popperfoto/Rolls Press), **21** (Chris Jackson), **23** (AFP/Desiree Martin), **25** (AFP Photo/Ben Borg Cardona), **26** (AFP/Desiree Martin); The National Archives pp. **16**, **19**; 082011
006318RP

North Wind Picture Archives p. **7**; Press Association Images p. **10** (PA Archive); The Phillips Collection, Washington, DC p. **12** (© ARS, NY and DACS, London 2010); TopFoto p. **9** (The Granger Collection, New York).

Cover photograph of African Americans who were part of the Great Migration to the north, 1918, reproduced with permission of Getty Images (Chicago History Museum).

We would like to acknowledge the following sources of material: pp. **6–11** from the National Women's History website, http://www.nwhm.org/education-resources/biography/biographies/phillis-wheatley. Accessed on November 19, 2010; p. **15** from "Obituary: Milt Hinton, Dean of Jazz Bassists, Is Dead at 90" by Peter Keepnews, *New York Times* website, December 20, 2000, http://www.nytimes.com/2000/12/21/nyregion/milt-hinton-dean-of-jazz-bassists-is-dead-at-90.html. Accessed November 19, 2010; p. **17** from the Moving Here Catalog, http://www.movinghere.org.uk/search/catalogue.asp?RecordID=76589. Accessed November 19, 2010; pp. **18**, **20** from the Moving Here Catalog, http://www.movinghere.org.uk/stories/Story_WMMHWolverhampton01; pp. **22–24** from "Migrants Risk All from Libyan Port" by Michael Buchanan, BBC News website, September 29, 2008, http://news.bbc.co.uk/2/hi/africa/7632429.stm. Accessed November 19, 2010; p. **26** from "A Migrant's Journey to Europe," BBC News website, September 12, 2006, http://news.bbc.co.uk/2/hi/talking_point/5331608.stm. Accessed November 19, 2010.

We would like to thank Professor Sarah Chinn for her invaluable help in the preparation of this book.

Contents

DAILY LIFE
Read here to learn what life was like for the children in these stories, and the impact that migrating had at home and at school.

NUMBER CRUNCHING
Find out the details about migration and the numbers of people involved.

Migrants' Lives
Read these boxes to find out what happened to the children in this book when they grew up.

HELPING HAND
Find out how people and organizations have helped children to migrate.

On the Scene
Read eyewitness accounts of migration in the migrants' own words.

Some words are printed in bold, **like this**. You can find out what they mean by looking in the glossary.

Many Reasons to Migrate

People **migrate**, or move to new homes, for many reasons. For some, a new place offers the promise of a better job or a better life for their family. Others flee wars or violence. Some **migrants** are forced to leave.

For hundreds of years, ships carried Africans to parts of the United States, South America, and the **Caribbean** to work as slaves. Later, laws were passed to end slavery. Today, the **descendants** of those slaves are a vital part of their societies.

Migration can also take place within a single country. Laws in southern U.S. states, for instance, kept African Americans out of schools and good jobs. Whites could even hurt or kill them, and the police would take no action.

In the early 1900s, African Americans began to leave the South to take their chances in northern states, where they could get an education and work and live without fear.

Migration continues

Africans are still on the move. Every day, **immigrants**—people born in a different country from the one they live in—step into the unknown to find a new home.

Michaëlle Jean was the governor general of Canada from 2005 to 2010. She is an immigrant from Haiti. She and her family left her home country for Quebec, Canada, when she was 11 years old.

Slavery: 1761

A girl was born in West Africa around 1753. When she was about eight years old, slave-takers kidnapped her from her home. The farther away they took her, the farther she left the life she knew behind her.

In the days of the **slave trade**, Africans often kidnapped people from other kingdoms or groups and forced them to walk to the coast of the Atlantic Ocean. There, non-African traders bought them as slaves. The ship owners would take the slaves across the Atlantic. On the other side, people bought the slaves and forced them to work for the rest of their lives.

Slave traders forced slaves to march from their homes to the coast.

Sailors put the girl on a ship called the *Phillis*. It landed in Boston, Massachusetts—in North America—in 1761.

Ship captains crowded as many Africans on board as possible so that they would have many slaves to sell.

DAILY LIFE

Africans forced onto slave ships entered a nightmare. Food ran short. Disease was common. The sailors beat the slaves and crammed them into a ship's **hold**. In the worst cases, the ships were so crowded that the slaves could barely move. Some Africans would jump into the sea rather than continue the journey.

Life with the Wheatley family

The Wheatley family looked to buy one of the slaves on the *Phillis*. Slaves cost money, but John Wheatley could afford them. He owned land, warehouses, a business, and a boat for carrying goods. His wife, Susannah, wanted a slave to help around the house and keep her company. They bought the skinny, sickly girl and named her Phillis, after the ship.

To the Wheatleys' surprise, Phillis quickly learned English. The family soon forgot about training Phillis for housework. Instead, Mary, the Wheatleys' daughter, taught Phillis religion and **literature**. Phillis began to write poems of her own. When asked to explain how a slave girl came to create poetry, John Wheatley said, "As to her own writing, her own curiosity led her to it."

In 1767, when Phillis was 14, a Rhode Island newspaper published one of her works. But her career was just getting started.

DAILY LIFE

The fact that Phillis learned to read and write was very unusual. Slave owners rarely educated slaves. Some considered Africans incapable of learning. Other people knew that an educated slave would often run away to freedom, rather than accept a life in slavery.

This statue of Phillis Wheatley is in Boston, Massachusetts.

A famous poet

In 1770 Phillis published a poem about a religious leader named George Whitefield. Her writing career took off. Newspapers printed Phillis's poems about figures in Great Britain and the 13 American **colonies**.

In May 1773, Phillis went to England. A British **countess** had promised to help have a book of her poems published. That summer, admirers in Britain made Phillis a minor celebrity. But Susannah Wheatley became ill. Phillis had to return to Boston before her book came out.

The city of Bristol, England, was on the route of the slave trade. These women attended a service in 2007 to mark 200 years since the end of Britain's role in that trade.

When Phillis's book reached the colonies, she became the first African American to publish a book of poetry in what would become the United States. A few years later, the American colonies began to fight for independence from Britain. Phillis tested her popularity by writing a poem that praised George Washington, a leader of the colonists. The colonists liked it, even if some of the British did not.

This portrait of Phillis Wheatley was printed in her book of poetry.

Phillis remained sickly. She was in poor health for the rest of her life. She planned a second book of poems, but it never came out. Phillis died in 1784. But she had already become a symbol of what African Americans could achieve.

Great African Migration: 1919

The American Civil War (1861–65) freed the slaves held in the United States. Over the next 50 years, however, white-led governments in the South took back the rights African Americans had gained after the war. In the early 1900s, African Americans began moving to northern cities. There were better jobs there. **Discrimination** there was not part of everyone's life, and it was less violent.

This painting by the African American artist Jacob Lawrence shows people boarding trains headed to the North.

Milton "Milt" Hinton was born in 1910 in Vicksburg, Mississippi. His mother gave him music lessons. Milt wanted to become a musician. One of Milt's uncles had moved to Chicago, Illinois. The uncle sent money to help buy a ticket for another family member. Many people did the same thing. Northern relatives helped whole families make the trip, one by one.

Milt's mother, Hilda, took her turn as a migrant. Milt stayed in Mississippi with his grandmother. In 1919 Hilda sent for them.

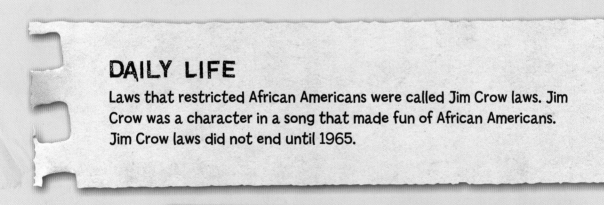

DAILY LIFE

Laws that restricted African Americans were called Jim Crow laws. Jim Crow was a character in a song that made fun of African Americans. Jim Crow laws did not end until 1965.

Jim Crow laws forced African Americans to remain separate from whites, even in waiting rooms at train stations.

WAITING ROOM FOR COLORED ONLY

→

BY ORDER POLICE DEPT.

Life in music

It rained as Milt and his grandmother waited for the train. The uncomfortable "blacks-only" train car lacked any place to change clothes. They made the trip north in wet clothes. When they finally got to Chicago, "we all looked so bad," Milt said.

African Americans formed groups to help recent migrants.

If You are a Stranger in the City

If you want a job   If you want a place to live
If you are having trouble with your employer
If you want information or advice of any kind

CALL UPON

The CHICAGO LEAGUE ON URBAN CONDITIONS AMONG NEGROES

3719 South State Street

Telephone Douglas 9098   T. ARNOLD HILL, Executive Secretary

No charges — no fees. We want to help YOU

Milt began violin lessons at the age of 13. In school he learned to play the saxophone, tuba, and cello, but he still preferred the violin. When he left school in 1929, however, there were few jobs for violinists. Milt turned to the large stringed instrument called the **bass**. He used his music training to develop a way of slapping the strings with his wrist.

Milt became a musician just as the bass was becoming a popular **jazz** instrument. His strong playing and good work habits soon got him jobs with many of the biggest jazz stars.

"The bass is a service instrument," he said. "You learn a lot of **humility**. You must be content in the background, knowing you're holding the whole thing together."

This is a photo of Milt Hinton in 2001.

Milton "Milt" Hinton

Milt's career included work on at least 600—and maybe 1,000—recordings. This was more than any other bass player in history. As he got older, he led his own band and taught at two colleges. He also became a noted photographer.

Caribbean Migration: 1964

Slaves taken from Africa first arrived in the Caribbean in the 1500s. In 1833 Great Britain finally ended slavery in the Caribbean countries it ruled. Islands in the Caribbean such as Jamaica, Barbados, and the Bahamas remained connected to Britain as parts of the **British Empire**.

During **World War II** (1939–45), Caribbean men served in Britain. There they saw that Britain offered more opportunities than they had at home. After the war, Britain badly needed workers. Caribbean men saw a chance to make money.

A ship called the *Empire Windrush* stopped in Jamaica in 1948. Hundreds of Jamaicans boarded for the trip to Britain.

This is what the passenger list for the *Empire Windrush* looked like.

Some of the *Empire Windrush* passengers meant to join the Royal Air Force. Others hoped to earn money and return home. From the day they landed, Britain became more of a **multicultural** country—that is, home to people from many cultures.

These are some of the first passengers to arrive in Britain on board the *Empire Windrush*.

On the scene

Steve Mitchell, a passenger on the *Empire Windrush*, took only the basics on the trip. "All I had was my bit of clothing, nothing else," he said. "I landed [in Britain] with £5 [about $8] and no tools, nothing else, couple of suits, . . . few shirts, no overcoat, no nothing, wasn't prepared for the cold weather."

17

The Caribbean migration continues

People streamed in from the Caribbean for years. In the early 1960s, Carmel Veronica Watson was staying with her grandmother in Manchester, Jamaica. Her parents had gone to Britain to work. Jamaica was warm and the fields were green. Carmel was free to explore as she liked. By the time she turned four in 1964, however, her grandmother was getting too old to handle a little girl. Carmel's parents sent for her.

She boarded an airplane with her brothers and sisters. "I was sad that I was leaving my family and close friends," she said. "With all my brothers and sisters together to comfort each other, I really felt secure on the flight. The only downside was the food, mashed potatoes, not for me."

HELPING HAND

In 1931 Harold Moody, a doctor born in Jamaica, founded the League of Coloured People in London. The League fought racial discrimination in Britain and demanded rights for people of color throughout the British Empire. The group faded after Moody's death in 1947, but it had helped prepare the way for the new multicultural Britain.

Many people on islands in the Caribbean had British habits and wanted to be a part of the "Mother Country." This included playing British sports such as cricket.

New country, new opportunity

Carmel's plane arrived at Heathrow Airport, near London, England, on September 21, 1964. Her father, George, was waiting. After greetings, the family began the trip north to Carmel's new home in Wolverhampton, England. The cold British weather shocked her. So did the trees without leaves, the sight of houses built so close together, and the smoke from the chimneys.

Carmel settled into her new neighborhood. The other children nearby came from many backgrounds. "Whitmore Reans was a very safe area," she said. "The neighbors whether black, white, Indian, or Irish looked after each other. This was a real community." She enjoyed going to a local school. At church, she learned to read poems in front of an audience.

Heathrow Airport was a cold and gray destination after sunny Jamaica.

Carmel Veronica Watson

Carmel's mother had been a nurse. Carmel followed the same path after high school. She worked in a hospital's **pediatric** (children's) intensive care unit for 20 years. Later, she earned a special nursing diploma that allowed her to work with the people of her community.

Carnival had a long history in the Caribbean. Afro-Caribbean communities started a carnival in London to celebrate their own cultures and traditions. In the last 50 years, the Notting Hill Carnival and similar events have become hugely popular with people of all cultures.

African Migration: Today

Today, not all African migration is **legal**. But some people are desperate enough to risk their lives and freedom to leave Africa.

Musa Korosa, a 21-year-old man from Nigeria, crossed the Sahara Desert to get to Zuwarah, Libya. Migrants used Zuwarah as a jumping-off point to go to Italy. Nigerians like Musa wanted to go to Europe for better jobs and to escape the **poverty** (poor conditions), hunger, violence, and bad government in their home country.

NUMBER CRUNCHING

Conditions in Europe encourage poor Africans to take risks to find a better life. An organization called the World Bank has made the following comparisons between conditions in Europe and sub-Saharan Africa (countries in Africa south of the Sahara Desert).

Age the average child will live:

Europe: 80 years
Sub-Saharan Africa: 47 years

Number of children in elementary school:

Europe: 98.9%
Sub-Saharan Africa: 65.7%

Number of Internet users:

Europe: 439.4 for every 1,000 people
Sub-Saharan Africa: 29 for every 1,000 people

Nigerian migrants in Libya were **illegal**. They received no food or help. Most had to secretly look for short-term jobs. Part of their pay went toward a fee to cross the Mediterranean Sea in a boat. In Zuwarah, men who owned old fishing boats charged migrants $1,460 per person for the journey. Musa raised the money in 2008. But the trip turned into a nightmare.

Migrants will take any form of transportation that they can find, including broken boats.

Desperate journey

Musa spent eight days in a boat with 350 people. During the trip, the engine gave out. Heavy seas battered those aboard. They ran out of food and water. Musa said that at least 135 people died.

Desperate Africans try other routes, too. Some aim for Malta, an island in the Mediterranean Sea. Others cross the Straits of Gibraltar to Spain.

One common migrant plan is to leave West Africa for the Canary Islands, which are Spanish islands just off the west coast of Africa. Migrant boats sometimes arrive on island beaches every day. Those aboard are often starving and thirsty.

Some boats sink on the way. Tens of thousands of Africans have died on boat journeys. Those who make it have trouble finding work and a place to stay. Many get sent back to their home countries. But the risks do not stop others. Some even make a second or third trip. Musa, for example, returned to Zuwarah to try again.

HELPING HAND

In 2003 the bodies of migrants were washed up on a beach near Rota, Spain. A local couple, Rafael Quiroz and Violeta Cuesta, discovered that many of the victims came from Hansala, a town in Morocco. They created the group Solidaridad Directa to make life better in Hansala, so that people do not risk their lives trying to escape in boats.

Migrants are sometimes held by the police. These migrants are in Malta.

Continuing Migration

Migration from Africa will not end anytime soon. Despite the risks and more efforts by Mediterranean countries to stop migrants, boats full of immigrants keep coming.

This boat of migrants has landed in the Canary Islands. "I and other Africans like myself feel we have no choice," a Nigerian man said. "I have to try and make a better life, I pray that God will see me through."

In recent years, many African immigrants have come to the United States. Between 1960 and 2007, their numbers increased from 35,355 to 1.4 million. Most of this increase came after 1990. New York City is home to many new African immigrants. Many Africans have also settled in California, Texas, Maryland, Virginia, and other states.

One downside to migration is that African nations lose many of their most educated and motivated people. That makes it hard to improve the situation in Africa. Worse still, the poverty, violence, and lack of jobs in several African countries encourage yet more people to leave. Until these things change, Africans will keep migrating to other lands—legally and illegally.

NUMBER CRUNCHING

The following are the top countries of origin for legal and illegal African immigrants to the United States and United Kingdom.

United States (2009), estimated

Nigeria	185,787
Egypt	136,648
Ethiopia	134,547

United Kingdom (2005)

South Africa	140,201
Kenya	129,356
Nigeria	88,105

Mapping Migration

Some of the people in this book had to leave their home, family, and friends. They may have had long and difficult journeys. Their experiences as children made them into the people they became as adults.

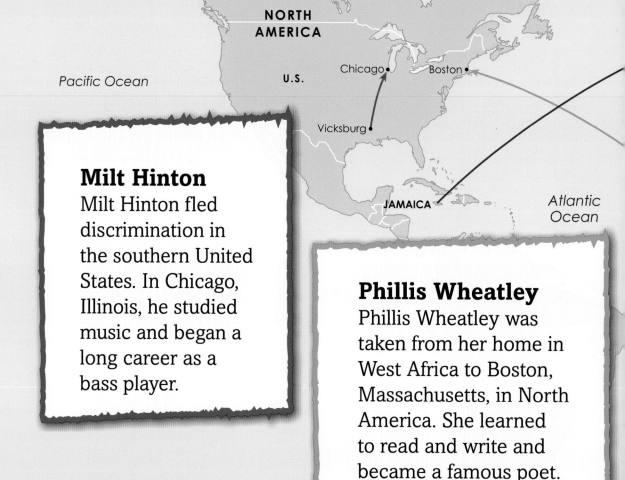

NORTH AMERICA

Pacific Ocean

U.S.

Chicago

Boston

Vicksburg

JAMAICA

Atlantic Ocean

Milt Hinton
Milt Hinton fled discrimination in the southern United States. In Chicago, Illinois, he studied music and began a long career as a bass player.

Phillis Wheatley
Phillis Wheatley was taken from her home in West Africa to Boston, Massachusetts, in North America. She learned to read and write and became a famous poet.

Arctic Ocean

ASIA

Carmel Veronica Watson

A native of Jamaica, Carmel Veronica Watson moved to Great Britain at age four. She became a pediatric nurse.

London

EUROPE

ITALY

•Zuwarah

LIBYA

Musa Korosa

Nigerian migrant Musa Korosa almost died on a dangerous boat journey from Libya to Italy. Thousands of Africans make similar trips every year.

NIGERIA

AFRICA

Indian Ocean

Glossary

bass large, stringed musical instrument with a deep sound. It may also be called a double bass, upright bass, or acoustic bass.

British Empire group of countries, islands, and territories governed by Great Britain from the 1500s until the 1990s

Caribbean islands off the coast of Central and South America

colony part of the world controlled by a country a long way away. Britain had colonies in America until the 1700s. Other parts of the world were British colonies into the 1900s.

countess British noblewoman; the wife of a count or earl

descendant relative descended from an older ancestor. A child is a descendant of his or her parents, grandparents, great-grandparents, and so on.

discrimination mistreating or rejecting a person based on his or her race, religion, country of origin, or other factors

hold large part of a ship that holds goods below the deck

humility state of being humble and modest

illegal outside or against the law

immigrant someone who comes in to live in another country

jazz music style known for strong rhythm and group playing

legal obeying the law

literature various forms of writing, such as poetry, stories, and plays

migrant person who moves from one place to another

migrate leave one's home to live somewhere else

multicultural "many cultures." Multicultural countries such as the United States have citizens with ancestors from many places.

pediatric having to do with children, usually in a medical sense

poverty poor conditions, often including lack of money to spend on food, clothes, housing, and education

slave trade system that kidnapped, transported, bought, and sold slaves

World War II war that took place between 1939 and 1945. In Europe the United Kingdom, Soviet Union, United States, and other countries fought against Germany and Italy.

Find Out More

Books

Gregson, Susan R. *Phillis Wheatley* (Let Freedom Ring). Mankato, Minn.: Bridgestone, 2002.

Halpern, Monica. *Moving North: African Americans and the Great Migration* (Crossroads America). Washington, D.C.: National Geographic, 2006.

Herr, Melody. *African Roots* (World Black History). Chicago: Heinemann Library, 2010.

Herr, Melody. *The Slave Trade* (World Black History). Chicago: Heinemann Library, 2010.

Spilsbury, Louise. *Moving People: Migration and Settlement* (Geography Focus). Chicago: Raintree, 2006.

Websites

www.inmotionaame.org
In Motion: The African-American Migration Experience

www.phillipscollection.org/migration_series/index.cfm
Jacob Lawrence: Migration Series

www.milthinton.com
Milt Hinton Official Site

www.movinghere.org.uk/galleries/histories/caribbean/caribbean.htm
Moving Here: Caribbean Migration Histories

www.usnationalslaverymuseum.org
U.S. National Slavery Museum

Places to visit

Museum of the African Diaspora
685 Mission Street
San Francisco, California 94105
Tel: (415) 358-7200

DuSable Museum of African American History
740 East 56th Place
Chicago, Illinois 60637
Tel: (773) 947-0600

Index